The Life for the Preaching of
THE HIGH GOSPEL

Witness Lee

Living Stream Ministry
Anaheim, CA • www.lsm.org

First Edition, April 1994.

ISBN 978-0-87083-776-0

Published by

Living Stream Ministry
2431 W. La Palma Ave., Anaheim, CA 92801 U.S.A.
P. O. Box 2121, Anaheim, CA 92814 U.S.A.

Printed in the United States of America

15   16   17   18   19   /   10   9   8   7   6   5

CONTENTS

PREFACE

This book is composed of messages given by Brother Witness Lee in Los Angeles, California on April 8 through 11, 1971.

CHAPTER ONE

MAN AS THE CENTER OF THE UNIVERSE

Scripture Reading: Gen. 1:26-28; Psa. 8:3-9; Heb. 2:5-9, 16

The burden of this book can be expressed in the following five statements:

Man is the center of the universe.
Christ is the meaning of human life.
The church is the expression of Christ.
The church life is the real communal life.
Go therefore and disciple all the nations.

MAN—THE CENTER OF GOD'S ETERNAL PURPOSE

The Bible is the divine revelation. It unveils to us not only God but even more, the purpose of God. In fundamental Christianity most of the messages are concerning man's personal salvation. It is difficult to hear anything on God's purpose. I hope that all of us can see what the purpose of God is.

If we want to see God's purpose, we must come to the divine book, the Holy Bible. The center of God's eternal purpose is man. According to the Bible and even according to scientific study, it is clear that man is the center of the universe. The universe is composed of the heavens, the earth, and millions of things created by God. The sun is the center of our solar system, but this solar system is just a small part of one galaxy, and there are millions of galaxies in the universe. We have to realize what the center of God's universe is. From God's Word we see that the center of God's universe is man. If there were no human life on this earth, the universe would become meaningless.

The Bible says in Genesis 1 that God first created the heavens and then the earth. After this He created all the things of life. He began with the creation of the things of the lowest form of life, the life that is without consciousness, which is the plant life. Following this, God created the animals. The animal life is higher than the plant life because the animal life is a life with consciousness. Eventually, God created the human life. Therefore, we have the plant life as the lowest life, the animal life as the higher life, and then the human life as the highest life of all the created things.

Suppose that there were no life in this universe—no plants, no animals, and no human life. What kind of universe would that be? Would you like to live in a place without any green things or without any animals? Surely no one would like to live in such a place. Without life, the universe would become meaningless. God, however, created all kinds of life—the plant life, the animal life, and the human life. The different kinds of plant life—the trees, the flowers, and the grass—are for beauty. New Zealand is really a beautiful land because it is so green. It is beautiful because of the abundance of life.

In addition to the plant life, there are the different kinds of animal life. The plant life is for beauty, and the animal life is to satisfy man's interest. This is why many people like to have a dog or a cat in their home. Without the human life, there would be no one to enjoy the beauty of the plant life and the stimulation of the animal life. Man is the one who manages and enjoys these created lives. This is why God did not create man first. He first created the plant life and then the animal life. Then He created man to enjoy and to exercise dominion over all things. By this we can see that man is the center of the universe. Without man, there is no meaning in the whole universe. The heavens and the earth, with the plant life and the animal life, become meaningless without man as the center.

MAN BEING GOD'S EXPRESSION AND REPRESENTATIVE

Man is the center and meaning of the universe because God has fully entrusted man with His purpose. God did not commit Himself to any of the millions of other created items.

He committed Himself only to man and entrusted man with His purpose. After He created the heavens and the earth, with the plant and animal lives, God had a conference in Himself with the three persons of the Godhead—the Father, the Son, and the Spirit. Genesis 1:26 says, "God said, Let Us..." Notice the plural pronoun *Us*. This is very meaningful. There is only one God, but God said, "Let Us." This indicates that there was a conference in the Godhead. God said, "Let Us make man in Our image, according to Our likeness." God had this kind of conference only for creating man. In this conference of the Godhead, a decision was made to create man in His image and according to His likeness.

The second half of Genesis 1:26 says, "And let them have dominion over the fish of the sea and over the birds of heaven and over the cattle and over all the earth and over every creeping thing that creeps upon the earth." This shows us that the decision made in the conference of the Godhead was not only to create man in God's image but also to give man the divine authority, the dominion, the ruling power, the reigning authority, over all living things. Moreover, God gave man the authority to rule over the earth and even to subdue and conquer the earth (v. 28).

We should declare, "Hallelujah! I am not a small thing, because I was created according to the counsel of the Godhead. I was created in God's image, and I have His authority entrusted to me to rule over all things." You should tell the animals that you have authority over them. If you do this, you will see yourself according to God's viewpoint. This does not mean that you will be proud, but that you will respect yourself as a person who was made in the image of God to have His divine authority over all things.

We human beings forget who we are. We do not regard ourselves as being higher than the animals, as those who have authority over the animals. But we have to realize that we are higher than the animals. We can tell all the animals, "I am much higher than you. You don't have the image of God, but I do. You don't have the authority of God, but I do. Not only so, I have the authority over you. You have to listen to me." We should praise the Lord for His creation of us in His image and His entrusting us with His authority. What a wonder this is!

God's purpose is to make man first His expression and then His representative. The image of God is for us to express God, and the authority of God is for us to represent Him. We are the expression of God and also the representative of God on this earth. What a position and commission we have! Especially the young people among us have to stand on this position and realize God's commission to man. Then they will know that they should always conduct themselves as God's expression and God's representative. We are the image of God and have the divine authority over all things. This shows us that man is the center of the universe. We need to go to the Lord to praise Him for His purpose with us. We need to praise Him for creating us in His image so that we may express Him and for entrusting us with His divine authority so that we may represent Him.

What are you doing here on this earth? If you realize that you were created in the image of God to express Him and that you have been entrusted with His authority to represent Him, this will revolutionize your whole life. Your life will become much more meaningful. You will never be disappointed. Of course, to be saved is wonderful, and we should praise the Lord for this. But we also have to praise the Lord for God's purpose. God saved you for His own purpose. Thus, we all have to say, "Hallelujah for the Lord's purpose!"

At the beginning of this chapter in the Scripture Reading, we have listed three portions from the divine Word: Genesis 1, Psalm 8, and Hebrews 2. Genesis 1 says that God decided to make man in His own image and to have man entrusted with His authority. But we know that after Genesis 1, man became fallen and lost such a position. After the fall of man, however, there is Psalm 8. The psalmist said, "When I see Your heavens, the works of Your fingers, / The moon and the stars, which You have ordained, / What is mortal man, that You remember him, / And the son of man, that You visit him?" (vv. 3-4; cf. Heb. 2:6). Notice that the psalmist did not say, "What are the angels?" Instead, he said, "What is mortal man?" While the psalmist was considering and looking at the heavens, he saw the moon and the stars. Seemingly, he should have had an appreciation for the angels. But instead of appreciating the angels, he said, "What is mortal man?" He looked at the heavens, the moon, and the stars, but he did not appreciate anything in the heavens. Rather, he appreciated man on this earth and wondered what man is.

Today the scientists are greatly concerned with the moon and the stars. The United States spent much money and effort to send a man to the moon. Even the psalmist was considering the moon and the stars, yet the Spirit turned him to man on this earth. We should not focus our attention on the heavens with the moon and the stars. Instead, we should focus our attention on the earth with man as the center. "O Jehovah our Lord, / How excellent is Your name / In all the earth" (Psa. 8:1). Note that the psalmist did not say that Jehovah's name is excellent in all the heavens, but "in all the earth."

My burden is to help the young people realize the preciousness of man in the eyes of God, not only at the time of man's creation but also after his fall. Everything on this earth is a mess. Due to the fall, the earth has become a tragedy. This is why man is always looking to the heavens. If the young people could fly away from this earth, surely they would do it. But God did not give us the capacity to fly away. He wants us to stay on this earth. This may not be our choice, but this surely is our destiny. We have to be on this earth. Even after the fall, God's interest is still on this earth. When we look at the heavens, the moon, and the stars, God would turn our spirit to look at man on this earth. We have to say from our spirit, "What is man?"

In order to see what man is, we need the entire sixty-six books of the Bible. Man is wonderful and meaningful. The Bible is a divine book that reveals to us not only God but also man. Do you know who you are? If you want to know who you are, you need to know the Bible. You have to say, "I am God's expression and God's representative. I am a person created in the image of God and entrusted with the divine authority." We all have to know this. This should not merely be a saying, a doctrine, or a teaching. This must be our practice. Day by day we should behave ourselves as those who always bear the image of God as God's expression and who have been committed with the divine authority as God's representative. This is God's purpose for man, and even after man's fall, God did not give up His purpose.

In order to accomplish His purpose, God Himself became a man. He identified Himself with man. He made Himself one with man. He came into man to be a man. Do you know what it means to be saved? To be saved, strictly speaking, is to have God incarnated into you to be one with you. To be saved is not just to be forgiven of your sins. To be saved is to have God identified with you, to have God incarnated in you, to have God become one with you.

By incarnation God brought Himself into man. Then by resurrection God brought man into Himself. Now there is a man in the heavens who is the mingling of divinity with humanity. He is a man altogether one with God. To be saved is to receive this man into you. Now that you are saved, you are a real VIP. You are truly a very important person. My burden in this chapter is to uplift you. You have to see how high you are. You have to see that you are a person on such a high level.

In the ancient times, people spoke with pride of their belonging to a royal family. But do you know that today we belong to a family that is even higher than any so-called royal family? We belong to the divine family. We are such wonderful persons, the VIPs on this earth. Jesus is not only our Savior but also a divine man, a God-man. He is the very God incarnated to be one with man. Today we have Jesus in us. He is mingled and blended with us, and we are a part of Him. This makes us VIPs in this universe.

If all the human beings were taken away from this earth, I believe that even God Himself would feel pitiful. But praise the Lord, there are human beings on this earth. Yet these human beings have become fallen. Look at the situation of today's world. Without the Christians, without those of us who realize that we are VIPs, what would the situation of the world be today? If there are many VIPs in a city, that city will have a great change. Before we began to meet at the

Elden meeting hall in Los Angeles, that area was really dark, morally speaking. But since the church began to meet there, that area has become greatly improved. If the church would have a great increase in number, just consider what kind of situation that would create. Hence, we need to go and disciple the nations.

I have a deep burden that some day in Los Angeles and in many other big cities, there will be Christian meetings that are not according to the old religion but according to the Lord's recovery. There will be meetings in many places without any religious forms. I look to the Lord that some day He will work this out for gaining people. The Lord is going to carry this out through the young generation. This cannot be worked out through old religion. The Lord is through with old religion with its religious forms and ordinances. The Lord is going to do something new.

The age has been turned from religion to Christ, from doctrines to the Spirit, from the forms and rituals to the new and living way. The young people are a greatly blessed generation. The Lord is going to do something new with the young generation. Forget about your background. Forget about what you obtained, what you saw, and what you received from the past. You have to realize that today is the day for the Lord to fulfill His purpose in a marvelous way, a way which has never been seen or heard before. May the Lord bless all of us.

CHAPTER TWO

CHRIST AS THE MEANING OF HUMAN LIFE

(1)

Scripture Reading: Gen. 1:26-28; Matt. 3:2; 5:3, 10, 48; 6:9-10, 31-33; Rom. 14:17; Rev. 11:15; 2 Tim. 2:12

In the previous chapter we saw that man is God's expression and His representative with His authority. In His creation God made man in His image and entrusted man with His dominion (Gen. 1:26-28). We have these two words: *image* and *dominion*. Image is a matter of life, whereas dominion is a matter of authority. Thus, we have the divine life and the divine authority involved here. Since man was created in the image of God, this means that man was meant to have God's life. And since God entrusted man with His dominion, this means that man was meant to have the authority of God. To express God we need the divine life. To represent God we need the divine authority.

However, man became fallen. Therefore, God Himself came to be a man named Jesus. Jesus was a wonderful man, and today, even in His resurrection, He is still a man. He is a man in the heavens. When Stephen was being stoned to death in his martyrdom, he saw "the heavens opened up and the Son of Man standing at the right hand of God" (Acts 7:56). Thus, today Christ in the heavens is still a man. But we have to realize that this is not all. After Christ was resurrected from the dead and ascended to the heavens, He came down as the life-giving Spirit (1 Cor. 15:45b) and as the Spirit of power (Acts 1:8).

This Spirit, who is Jesus Himself, is now waiting for all the fallen human beings to receive Him. As soon as a person receives Him, this wonderful One, Jesus, immediately enters into him. This means that this person is saved. To be saved simply means to have Christ coming into us.

REPENTING FOR THE KINGDOM OF THE HEAVENS

We all know that it is not a small thing to have Christ come into us. However, there is something deeper than this. The opening word of the gospel of the kingdom is *repent*. We need to repent for the kingdom of the heavens (Matt. 3:2) because we have fallen from the dominion of God. Therefore, we need to come back. We need to have a real turn from the fallen state to the original state. We have to leave the fallen situation and turn to God's dominion again. This dominion is simply the kingdom of the heavens.

Christians today talk a lot about gospel preaching, but what do we preach as the gospel? We may say that we preach Christ. This is right, but it is still inadequate. The gospel preached at the beginning of the New Testament was, "Repent, for the kingdom of the heavens has drawn near." We were made in the image of God, and we were entrusted with God's dominion, but we became fallen. Now we have to return to God's dominion; then we will have His image again.

FOUR CATEGORIES OF PEOPLE

I wish to put these things in a more simple and practical way. Look at the situation of today's human life and society. People all over the world are materialistic. They are busily working to gain material things for a good living. They want to have better food, a better house, a better car, and better clothing. All the time they are seeking for something better. But eventually what they seek for becomes bitter. America today is a materialistic country. The materialistic people are the first category of people we see in today's society.

Another category of people is composed of those who are trying to be good, to be moral. When people become materialistic, they do not care much for morality. Therefore, generally speaking, materialistic people are not so moral. But today on this earth there are some people who are highly moral.

Then we have a third category of people—the religious

people. In Christianity, to be religious is really wonderful; it is to be formal and scriptural. Hence, in a general sense, the religious people are not only better than the materialistic people but also better than the moral people.

The fourth category of people, the highest category, is the spiritual people. To be spiritual is to be in the spirit. Therefore, compared to the previous three categories of people, the spiritual people are really much better.

THE KIND OF PEOPLE GOD WANTS

Now let us ask what kind of people God wants. Of course, God does not want a group of materialistic people; nor does He want a group of moral or religious people. Furthermore, strictly speaking, God's intention is not to have a group of so-called spiritual people. God wants a group of people who would return to His dominion.

SEEKING FIRST GOD'S KINGDOM
AND HIS RIGHTEOUSNESS

In Matthew 6:31-33 the Lord said, "Therefore do not be anxious, saying, What shall we eat? or, What shall we drink? or, With what shall we be clothed? For all these things the Gentiles are anxiously seeking. For your heavenly Father knows that you need all these things. But seek first His kingdom and His righteousness, and all these things will be added to you." If you are always thinking about the matters of eating, drinking, and clothing, you are materialistic. The Lord told us to forget about these material things, which the Gentiles seek after all the time. Rather, we should seek first the kingdom of God and the righteousness of God.

We have seen that the kingdom of God is the dominion of God, but what is the righteousness of God? To be righteous is to be right with God and to be right according to what God is. God is love, yet you hate others. This is wrong. Since God is love, you also should love others. This is right. God is faithful, yet you are unfaithful. This is wrong. Since God is faithful, you also should be faithful. Then you are right. God is honest, yet you are dishonest. This is not right. To be honest is to be right according to what God is. Therefore, we can see that to be righteous simply means to be right according to God, not according to our concept. To be right according to God is to be completely agreeable with God.

The young people should consider what they are seeking today. They should be seeking to be brought back to God's dominion, God's ruling. Day by day you should be brought under God's ruling. Furthermore, while you are seeking God's kingdom, you should also seek His righteousness. This simply means that you have to return to God's dominion and to get yourself completely agreeable with God. If we want to be agreeable with God, we need to be born of God. We need to have His life and become His children.

People talk much about the so-called Sermon on the Mount. But we must see that unless we become the children of God, we cannot practice the Sermon on the Mount. The Sermon on the Mount is not for worldly people, the unbelievers, but for the children of the Father. This is indicated in Matthew 5:48, where the Lord said, "You therefore shall be perfect as your heavenly Father is perfect." We are His children, and He is our Father. We have His life. Therefore, we can be perfect as He is. For us to be perfect as the Father is perfect simply means that we have the Father's image, or in other words, that we express the Father.

However, there is still one crucial thing, and that is whether or not we are in the dominion of God. This is why the Lord Jesus told us to seek first the kingdom of God and His righteousness. It is not righteousness first but the kingdom. First, we need to seek the kingdom, and then spontaneously we will have righteousness. As we have seen earlier, righteousness simply means to be right according to God, to be completely agreeable with God. This is to be perfect as God the Father is perfect.

I would like to stress again that what God wants is not moral people, religious people, or even so-called spiritual people. What God wants are people who remain under His dominion. As long as you are under God's dominion, God's authority, all things will be under your dominion, your authority. If you are going to represent God, you need to be in God's dominion.

In human society there are many deceiving things. The material things are deceptions. Thus, people are constantly anxious, saying, "What shall we eat? What shall we drink? With what shall we be clothed?" All these *whats* are deceptions. The Lord Jesus told us that these are things sought after by the Gentiles. We have to forget about these things and seek God's kingdom and God's righteousness.

But how about our living? In Matthew 6:32 the Lord Jesus told us that our heavenly Father knows that we need all these things, and then in verse 33 He spoke a word as a promise: "Seek first His kingdom and His righteousness, and all these things will be added to you." Do you really believe that the heavenly Father will take care of your living? I have been believing in the heavenly Father's care for many years. We have to believe in the Lord's word. If we seek the kingdom of God and the righteousness of God, He will give us His kingdom and His righteousness. In addition, He will give us all the things that we need.

I realize that it is not so easy for the young people to believe that the Father will take care of all their needs. Many of you are worried about your future. I am afraid that many of you are also anxious about your marriage. A sister may wonder, "What kind of husband should I have?" A brother may consider, "What kind of wife is good for me?" Let me tell you honestly that without God, you can never have a good husband or a good wife. This is why today there are so many divorces. Learn to leave everything to God.

When I was young in the Lord's ministry, the young people considered me as a teacher of the Word of God and also as one who was experienced in the matter of marriage, since I was already married. Therefore, they used to come to me for advice concerning their marriage. I gave them the best instructions that I had collected, and they tried to apply them. But eventually, I found out that these good instructions did not work.

Now when the young people ask me about whom they should marry, I answer, "I don't know. Only the Lord knows." I can only tell them that if they feel led of the Lord to marry that sister or that brother, then they should just go ahead and do it. I cannot say whether that brother or that sister is good or not. I do not know. Only the Lord knows. Young brothers and sisters, you have to trust in the heavenly Father for your future, including your marriage. Only He knows. Your destiny is not in your hand; it is in His hand. Leave all things to Him. Just learn to say, "Hallelujah! I have a heavenly Father taking care of me in all ways."

Therefore, do not be deceived any longer by material things. Surely you need to study to get an education or learn a trade. But you should not be deceived by these things. We should not be preoccupied by these things. We do not seek these things first. We first seek the kingdom, the dominion, of God. We also seek to have His righteousness, to be right with Him, to be agreeable with Him. We desire to be perfect as He is perfect. We desire to bear His image and be under His authority all the time. We are not here to be moral, religious, or spiritual. We care only for one thing, that is, to be under His authority and to be agreeable with Him all the time.

We care only to be under God's authority. If God gives you the command to shout in the meeting, you should shout. If you say, "Oh, maybe it's not good to shout so loudly. I should take care of others," this is to be religious. I care only to be under the Lord's dominion. I care only to be right and agreeable with the Lord. We should not be deceived by religious things, which are even more deceiving than material and moral things.

Even the desire to be spiritual can be a kind of deceiving. This is why I feel compelled by the Lord to tell you these things. The Lord has no intention to gain a group of people who are "spiritual." Rather, His intention is to have a group of people who are under His authority, who are always right according to the Lord and completely agreeable with the Lord.

You can be like this only by taking Him as your person. Take Him not only as your life but also as your person. Then day by day you can declare to the whole universe, "It is no longer I who live, but it is Christ who lives in me" (Gal. 2:20a). Then you have the real righteousness. You are right and agreeable with the Lord because you are Christ Himself. It is no more you, but it is Christ, so you have the righteousness under God's authority.

I have no intention to advise you to do this or not to do that. My burden is to help you realize that today the Lord is going to get a people, mainly of the young generation, who do not care for anything material, anything moral, anything religious, or anything spiritual. Of course, they also do not care for anything immoral, unreligious, or unspiritual. They care only for God's dominion and God's image. Brothers and sisters, the Lord is going to gain a people of the young generation who truly seek first God's kingdom and God's righteousness. Eventually, God will give them the material things that they need, and they will be the most moral and spiritual people. But if you are just seeking after spirituality, you might be wrong. Today what you should seek after is not religion or spirituality. You need to seek the kingdom of God as well as His righteousness. We all need to be under His dominion and bear His image continually.

Matthew 5:3 says, "Blessed are the poor in spirit, for theirs is the kingdom of the heavens." Then verse 10 says, "Blessed are those who are persecuted for the sake of righteousness, for theirs is the kingdom of the heavens." First, you need to be poor in your spirit. Do not consider that you know something or have something. You have to prostrate yourself, bow down, before the Lord, saying, "Lord, I have nothing, and I know nothing. I don't like to retain or hold on to anything old in my spirit. I like to be poor in my spirit." If so, yours is the kingdom of the heavens.

You also have to be ready to suffer, to be persecuted, for the sake of righteousness, that is, for the sake of being right according to God, agreeable with God. If you want to be right according to God, you will be persecuted, because the whole world, which lies in the evil one (1 John 5:19) and is filled with unrighteousness, will rise up against you. In a sense, if you are seeking to be religious, many people will admire and welcome you. Also, in a sense, if you are seeking to be spiritual, many people will appreciate and speak well of you. But if you are seeking to be right with the Lord, to be right according to God, be prepared to be opposed and perse-cuted. But praise the Lord, the kingdom of the heavens is yours. You are in the kingdom of the heavens and are under God's dominion where you have the righteousness of God.

Today what the Lord is doing is gaining such a people as a preparation for His coming back to take over the earth. Then Revelation 11:15 will be fully fulfilled: "The kingdom of the world has become the kingdom of our Lord and of His Christ, and He will reign forever and ever." We will also reign with Him (2 Tim. 2:12).

Chapter Three

CHRIST AS THE MEANING OF HUMAN LIFE

(2)

Scripture Reading: John 6:57; 14:19-20, 23; 15:4-5; Gal. 2:20a; Eph. 3:16-17; Phil. 1:20b-21

I would like to impress us again with the five wonderful statements mentioned in the first chapter that specifically express the burden of this book. First, man is the center of the universe. Second, Christ is the meaning of human life. Third, the church is the expression of Christ. Fourth, the church life is the real communal life. Fifth, go therefore and disciple all the nations.

GOD'S NEED FOR US AND OUR NEED FOR CHRIST

In this chapter my burden is to share with you that God needs us. God needs man, and man needs Christ. Without man, God cannot fulfill His purpose. Without man, God can do nothing. On the other hand, we also have to say, "Without Christ, I can do nothing." Without us, God can do nothing, and without Christ, we can do nothing. God needs us, and we need Christ. We are here for God, and Christ is here for us.

If we were not for God and if we did not have Christ for us, we would be miserable and pitiful. Unfortunately, this is the real situation of today's world. The people in the world are not for God, and they do not have Christ for them. They just go along by themselves and by trusting themselves. But we Christians are different in that we are for God, and we have Christ for us. Do you have a genuine realization that you are for God and that you have Christ for you? If you really do, you will be on fire, and you will go and tell people this.

TAKING CHRIST AS OUR LIFE

We said in the preceding chapters that God has a purpose. God's purpose is to express Himself and also to deal with His enemy. To carry out His twofold purpose, God needs man to be His expression and to subdue His enemy. But how can man do this? Humanly speaking, we may be incapable of doing many things, but all of us can breathe, drink, and eat. Even the little babes know how to do these things. There is no need for anyone to teach them. In the same manner, we are incapable in the spiritual realm, but we can breathe in Christ (John 20:22), drink Christ (4:14; 7:37), and take Christ in as our food (6:35, 51, 57). Christ is the air, the breath; Christ is the water, the drink; and Christ is the bread, the food. Therefore, we all can take Christ in. God has no intention for us to express Him by ourselves or to do anything for Him by ourselves. God's intention is that we express Him and do things for Him by taking Christ as our life (Col. 3:4; John 6:57; 14:19).

There are two big mistakes—one made by the worldly people and the other by the Christians. The big mistake of the worldly people is that they do nothing for God. The Christians, on the other hand, try to do something for God by themselves. This also is a big mistake. The right way for us is to do something for God not by ourselves but by taking Christ as our life. The Lord Jesus said, "Apart from Me you can do nothing" (15:5b). Yet the apostle Paul said, "I am able to do all things in Him who empowers me" (Phil. 4:13). Without Christ, we can do nothing. But with Christ and in Christ, we are able to do all things. In John 14:20 the Lord told the disciples, "In that day you will know that I am in My Father, and you in Me, and I in you." Hence, we are not without Christ. We have Christ, and we are in Christ.

In today's human society there is nothing except vanity and misery because people are on the wrong way. They have nothing to do with God. The Christians, however, are trying to do something for God by themselves. Now, at the end of this age, the Lord is going to recover something mainly through the younger generation. Therefore, you young people all have to learn how to be for God by taking Christ as your life. If I ask you what you are doing here, you should not say that you are here studying or working. Rather, you have to say, "I am here in Southern California for God!" What are the young people doing here? They are here for God! By what way? By taking Christ as their life! This means that they are breathing Christ, drinking Christ, and eating Christ.

Without us, God can do nothing, and without Christ, we can do nothing. We are vessels for God who need to take Christ as our life. How wonderful it is that we are good for taking Christ as our life! The animals were not created for taking Christ, but we were. We all are qualified to take Christ. If you truly realize this, you will go out to tell people that they are good and qualified for taking Christ. Christ is our life (Col. 3:4), and the eternal life is nothing less than Christ Himself (John 3:15-16, 36; 14:6a).

TAKING CHRIST AS OUR PERSON

For the past years we have been stressing Christ as our life, but in recent days the Lord has shown us that He is also a person. In John 15:4a He says, "Abide in Me and I in you." You as a person abide in Christ, and He as a person abides in you. Christ is a person. He is not merely power, strength, might, or life, but a person. Within a tree there is life, but the tree is not a person. Within a motor there is power, but the motor is not a person. But within a man there is life and power, and even the more, he is a person. Christ to us is not only life and power but also a person abiding in us (vv. 4a, 5a; 14:23).

Ephesians 3:17a says, "That Christ may make His home in your hearts." A person needs a home. Christ desires to make His home in our hearts. This means that this Christ who is making home in our hearts is a person. God's intention is that we human beings take Christ as our person. This means that we have to live, not by ourselves but by Christ as our person (Gal. 2:20a; Phil. 1:20b-21; John 6:57; 14:19).

Suppose we have a young man and a young lady who are going to get married. They are two beings with two persons. How can the two of them become one being? In many weddings the head of the bride is covered. This signifies that the two persons become one since the wife is willing to have her head covered. As a wife you have to realize that, according to God's economy, your head has to be covered. This does not mean that the man as the head has authority and that the wife is miserable in losing all her rights. Rather, it is a matter of love. It means that the wife loves her husband to such an extent that she is willing to give herself up. She is willing to give up her person and take her husband as her person. As a living being, she does not live by her own person; she lives by her husband's person. This is real love.

Likewise, we need to give up our person and take Christ as our person. When we are willing to forget about ourselves and take Christ as our person, we will be rooted and grounded in love (Eph. 3:17b). We will say to the Lord, "O Lord Jesus, I just love You. You are so wonderful, good, nice, capable, and qualified. O Lord, You are so sweet and tender. I want to forget about myself and take You as my person."

Among the saints, the husband should not say to his wife, "Did you hear the message in the meeting tonight? Who is the head?" The wife may say, "Yes, I heard that. No doubt, you are the husband, so you are the head. But it's pitiful that I am a woman. Since I am your wife, I have no choice but to cover my head." This kind of wrong understanding concerning the husband being the head, the person, of the wife will lead to either separation or divorce. We must know that the wife's taking the husband as her person is a matter of love. When we take Christ as our person, it simply means that we love Him. We tell Him, "O Lord Jesus, You are so sweet and capable. Therefore, Lord, I just forget about myself, and I take You as my person." If I ask a sister why she is wearing a particular dress, she may say, "Because I like it." This is a failure. As a wife you should be able to say, "I wear this dress because my husband likes it." Suppose I ask a brother, "Why do you comb your hair that way?" His answer should be, "Because my Husband, the Lord who lives in me, likes it." This is what it means to take Christ as our person.

Let me share a living testimony with you. After I had given some messages concerning taking Christ as our person, a sister testified that in the past she had difficulty going to sleep at night. She used to pray earnestly, asking the Lord to help her go to sleep. But from the time that she understood the real meaning of taking Christ as her person, she began to change her way of prayer. She prayed in a simple way, saying, "Lord, do You want to sleep or not? If You want to sleep, then I sleep. If You don't want to sleep, then I don't sleep." She told us that after she prayed this way, she immediately went to sleep. This is a good example of what it means to take Christ as your person.

Recently, I checked with one of the young students. I said, "Brother So-and-so, after tonight's meeting, you are going to take a bus. How would you pray?" He said, "I will pray, 'Lord, which bus should I take?'" I told him that his prayer was a religious prayer and that it was wrong to pray that way. Then I told him, "When you go out of the meeting hall, you need to have a little talk with the Lord, saying, 'Lord, which bus are You going to take? If You take bus number one, I will take that too. If You take bus number two, I will also take the same bus.'" It is so simple to take Christ as our person.

Do not try to be holy, spiritual, or victorious. Forget about all these things. Always take Christ as your person. Always tell Him and tell the whole universe that now you are not living by yourself. You are living by Christ not only as your life but also as your person. It is so simple. I encourage all of you, the younger ones as well as the older ones, to try it. We need to be simplified. We have become complicated by Christian teachings. We were taught that we should be holy, but we need to forget about this. Instead, be so simple and go to the Lord. Just tell Him, "O Lord, You are not only my life but also my person. I am good and qualified for taking You as my person."

Wherever you are, whatever you do, and whatever you say, simply take Christ as your person. Suppose tomorrow you plan to go to the beach. You have to put this into practice and ask, "Lord, will You go to the beach tomorrow? Lord, if You go, I will go. If You do not go, neither will I. You are my person." It is so simple. If we all take Christ as our person, spontaneously we will express God, and we will also subdue the enemy.

We will conquer all the enemies and have a conquering life instead of a conquered life.

Just be simple. Learn to practice taking Christ as your person in all the things in your daily walk. In everything learn to take Christ as your person. Do not take this as a doctrine. Take this word and put it into practice in your daily living. Then you will see how prevailing it is. If you take Christ as your person, you will spontaneously express God and represent God. All day long the enemy will be under your feet. You will have a subduing life instead of a subdued life. This means that you will be victorious.

CHAPTER FOUR

CHRIST AS THE MEANING OF HUMAN LIFE

(3)

Scripture Reading: Gen. 2:9; John 1:4; 10:10b; 7:37-39; 6:63;
1 John 1:2; 5:11-12; Col. 3:4; 1 Cor. 15:45b; Rev. 21:6c; 22:1-2, 17;
7:17

SEEKING FIRST HIS KINGDOM
AND HIS RIGHTEOUSNESS

Before we continue with the matter of Christ as the meaning of human life, let us review some of the points covered in the preceding chapters. We have seen that man as the center of the universe is the expression of God and the representative of God. We have two wonderful words for these two points. For the first point the wonderful word is *image*. We have the image of God. The wonderful word for the second point is *dominion*. We have the dominion of God.

In the Gospel of Matthew, which is the book of the kingdom, we have the term *kingdom*—the kingdom of the heavens. The kingdom of the heavens simply equals the dominion of God. Hence, *kingdom* and *dominion* refer to the same thing. When man became fallen, he was fallen from the dominion, the kingdom, of God, not from the heavens. So man has to return to God's dominion, not to the heavens.

Dominion is an Old Testament term used in the first book of the Old Testament. But in the first book of the New Testament, the term used is *kingdom*. "Repent, for the kingdom...has drawn near" (Matt. 3:2). You have to realize that you are fallen from the dominion, the kingdom. Now you need to turn back to the dominion, the kingdom. Do not let your thoughts be so much on the heavens. Unfortunately, Christianity preaches too much on the heavens. But John the Baptist did not say, "Repent, for heaven has drawn near. Go back home to heaven." Rather, he told people to repent for the kingdom. The kingdom is the dominion from which you were fallen. Now you need to return to the very sphere from which you were fallen, that is, the kingdom, the dominion.

Then in the book of Matthew we also have the word *righteousness,* which equals the image of God in Genesis 1. To have the righteousness of God does not mean merely to be right with God but to be right according to what God is. To be right with God is one thing, and to be right according to God is another thing. The religious people stress the matter of being right with God but often neglect the matter of being right according to what God is. So what is the difference between these two things?

Let me give you a little illustration. Peter received the revelation of Christ as the Son of the living God (Matt. 16:16-17). He also saw the vision of the transfigured, glorified Jesus (17:1-5) and even had the experience of the outpoured Spirit on the day of Pentecost (Acts 2:1-41). Yet in Acts 10 Peter was so religious. He went up on the housetop to keep his prayer time. While he was praying, a trance came upon him (vv. 9-10). In his trance he saw a vision: "A certain vessel like a great sheet descending, being let down by four corners onto the earth, in which were all the four-footed animals and reptiles of the earth and birds of heaven" (vv. 11-12). These animals or beasts were considered common and unclean by the Jews according to the Old Testament ordinances. But a voice came to Peter, saying, "Rise up, Peter; slay and eat!" (v. 13). But what did Peter say? He said, "By no means, Lord" (v. 14).

By no means was according to Peter's religious concept. Peter did not behave in the right way that is according to God. Rather, he behaved rightly according to the religious concept that was passed down from his forefathers for many generations. But the Lord told him, "Eat!" The Lord seemed to be saying, "Peter, you should not be right according to your religion. You should be right according to Me. Today is the day of Christ, not of religion."

It is not easy to get away from your religious concept. Peter said no to the Lord three times (vv. 14-16). He was religious, but he was not in the Lord's dominion. He was in his own dominion. He did not care for what the Lord said. It was the Lord who spoke to him. That was not a voice from hell; that was a voice from heaven. Can you believe that Peter would even say no to the voice from heaven? If that were a voice which came from below, from the ground floor or the basement, to the housetop, it might have been right for Peter to say no. But that was a voice from heaven, and Peter disobeyed.

Brothers and sisters, you have to see that religion is deceitful. You do not know how much you have been deceived by your old religious concepts, nor have you realized how much you are preoccupied with the religion that you inherited from your forefathers. The material things and the moral things are deceitful, and the religious things are even more deceitful. I would even say that the spiritual things are the most deceitful.

It is easy for you to be clear that you are deceived by material things. But it is not so easy for you to realize that you can be deceived by religious things and even by spiritual things. Satan utilizes all things, whether material things, moral things, religious things, or spiritual things, to keep you away from God's dominion. It does not matter to Satan whether you are materialistic, moral, religious, or spiritual. The only thing he cares about is that you be kept away from God's dominion. As long as you are not in God's dominion, whatever you are or do is all right with Satan. Oh, how subtle the enemy is! Today the enemy not only uses material things but also utilizes religion and so-called spirituality to deceive you. He causes you to care only for being religious, for being godly, and for being spiritual, yet not to care for God's authority.

The Lord told Peter to "slay and eat!" Yet Peter said, "By no means, Lord, for I have never eaten anything common and unclean." No doubt, Peter was wrong, and there would have been no rescue for him if he had been wrong intentionally. But because he was wrong unintentionally, there was the rescue for him. Afterward, he became clear and saw that the age had changed. He began to realize that he should no longer care for his religious concepts. He should simply care for what the Spirit said. Eventually, he went to eat the unclean things. That means that he went to contact the family of Cornelius (vv. 17-33). To eat is to associate with people (vv. 13, 28). Cornelius and his relatives and intimate friends as Gentiles were considered unclean by the Jews. But Peter went to "eat" them, to associate with them, to preach the word of God to them.

When Peter went back to Jerusalem, those of the circumcision disputed with him, questioning him about his eating with the uncircumcised (11:2-3). Peter had acted wisely when he went to the house of Cornelius. He had six brothers from Joppa accompany him (10:23; 11:12), so there was a total of seven who went. Therefore, with the six brothers as witnesses to his word, Peter narrated the whole story to the brothers in Jerusalem and was vindicated of his way (vv. 4-18). This illustration shows us that we can be religious yet be outside of God's dominion. We have to be right day and night according to what God is and according to what God says, not according to our religious concept or opinion.

Thus, in Matthew we have the kingdom that equals God's dominion and the righteousness that equals God's image. Furthermore, in Matthew, in the so-called Sermon on the Mount, the Lord Jesus said, "You therefore shall be perfect as your heavenly Father is perfect" (5:48). The Lord did not say that we should be perfect according to what the law of Moses teaches. That we should be perfect as our heavenly Father is perfect means that we should be the expression of the Father. We are the children of the Father, so we have to be the same as the Father. To be the same as the Father is to express the Father. This is the expression, the image. Now you understand what the Lord meant when He said, "Seek first His kingdom and His righteousness" (6:33). This simply means that you need to seek the dominion of God and the image of God. This is to go back to the very beginning of the Bible. You became fallen from Genesis 1, so now you have to go back there. You became fallen from the dominion and the image of God, so now you need to return to the dominion and the expression of God.

The gospel of God is not a matter of repenting so that we may go to heaven or so that we may be forgiven of our sins. The thought of God's gospel is that we return to the original state from which we became fallen. Matthew, the first book of the New Testament, brings us back to Genesis, the first book of the Old Testament. We all have to go back to Genesis 1. What does this mean? It simply means to go back to God's original purpose. God's original purpose was to have man as His expression and as His representative. But from these two main points man became fallen. Now man needs to return to these two main points. For so many centuries Christianity has been short of this. But I do have the assurance and deep conviction within me that the Lord today is going to recover these two main points.

THE LORD'S NEED OF YOUNG PEOPLE
FOR HIS NEW MOVE

When the Lord Jesus came the first time, there was a strong religion. With that religion there was, first, the Holy Land. Then, within the Holy Land there was the holy city. Moreover, within that holy city there was the holy temple in which was the Holy Bible. People there were worshipping and serving God according to the Holy Scriptures in three holy things—in the holy temple, in the holy city, and in the Holy Land. In that kind of holy situation, the Lord Jesus came. Have you noticed that when the Lord Jesus came, He did not do anything according to those holy things? He did not bring people to the holy city or into the holy temple. Instead, Matthew tells us that when the Lord started His ministry, He went to "Galilee of the Gentiles" (4:12, 15). He did not go into the temple and call some of the praying priests to follow Him. Instead, He went to the Sea of Galilee. There He saw some fishermen, and among them were Peter and Andrew. Going on further, He saw James and John mending their nets. So the Lord called the fishermen and the menders to follow Him (vv. 18-22). But He did not bring them into the holy temple to worship God. Rather, sometimes He brought them to the mountain, and other times He brought them to the seashore. One time He gave Peter a lesson of faith by having him jump into the sea and walk on the water (14:28-29). Jesus did a lot of seemingly strange things outside of religion and against religion.

The Bible gives us a clear record, a picture, showing us how the religious people were zealous for God. Nevertheless, they were out-of-date. According to Luke there was an old sister, a prophetess, named Anna. She did not depart from the temple and was serving God with fastings and petitions night and day (2:36-37). She was absolutely for God. But for the actual carrying out of God's new move on the earth, the Lord had to go to Peter, a young man who was fishing in the sea, not praying in the temple.

There was another one, an old brother in Jerusalem named Simeon, who "was righteous and devout, waiting for the consolation of Israel" (v. 25). Both Anna and Simeon were absolutely for the Lord, but the Lord did not call them to follow Him. Instead, He went to the Sea of Galilee to call Peter, Andrew, James, and John, who were all young people. They were not like the holy Anna, praying in the temple all day long, nor were they like the holy Simeon, teaching people according to the prophecy of the Bible. Yet the Lord called these Galilean fishers to follow Him. The old holy people, holding the Holy Scriptures, were worshipping and serving in the holy temple, in the holy city, and in the Holy Land. But the Lord went to the seashore of Galilee of the Gentiles and called out two fishermen and two menders.

Brothers and sisters, today the situation is exactly the same as in that day. In today's Christianity there are many holy things—holy cathedrals, holy services, and holy days. I am convinced that this is why the Lord is going to the beaches, the parks, the street corners, the parking lots, etc., to gain the young people. You may say that these young people are hippies and are not holy, but the Lord says, "They are coming along with Me. They do not go along with you religious people. But they do go along with Me. I will never bring them into your religion. But I am bringing them back into the dominion of God. I don't care whether they have long hair or short hair, whether they are shaved or unshaved, whether they have bare feet or have shoes. I care for only one thing, that is, whether they are in God's dominion or not."

I believe that the Lord is going to move in a fast way. When the day of Pentecost came, three thousand were saved on that one day (Acts 2:41). On another day five thousand were saved (4:4). If one day in Southern California, ten thousand people, especially the young people, would turn to the Lord's dominion, it would not be a surprise to me. In this country today a great number of young people are rebellious toward the old way of life. Of course, this is not good for the families, the society, and the country. But the Lord is sovereign; all the nations are under Him. The United States was and still is a Christian country. But look at the situation today. If the young people of this generation were still stuck to the old way of living, it would be rather hard for them to be saved.

But today thousands of young people, many of whom are hippies, have been saved. They forget about the world and give up the old way of living. We do believe that the Lord will turn a great number of hippies to Himself. How can you bring them in? Do you bring them into the cathedrals, into the so-called church buildings? No! Go to meet with them on the beaches. If two or three hundred of the young saints have the feeling and the burden to go to the beach to meet, they should do it. You can bring with you the public-address system and broadcast the good news to everyone, asking them to come and join you in the church in Los Angeles.

We can never confine the Lord Jesus. Today the situation of Christianity is exactly the same as that in the ancient days of Judaism. My burden is to share with you that today the Lord Jesus is going to do a new thing with a new generation. Apparently, Anna and Simeon were not in that move, but they were absolutely for that move, and they prayed very much for it. I believe many elderly ones who are for the Lord are in the same position as Anna and Simeon. You have to pray night and day for the Lord's new move. Yet for the move itself, the Lord will use mostly the young people.

When the Lord was on earth, He used the fishermen and the menders, the Galileans. He used those who were not in the temple but in the boats on the sea, and He used those who were willing to jump into the water. The Lord Jesus came to the disciples, walking on the sea, and said to Peter, "Come." That means Peter had to jump into the water, and he did it. Suppose Peter would have said, "No, Lord, I won't jump into the water. Why can't I stay in the boat? To be in the boat is safe. It is the logical thing to do. Sooner or later I will come to You. You just wait awhile." Then he would have become a materialistic person, who was so rational, logical, and sound that he would not jump into the water but would stay in the boat and come to the Lord gradually. The Lord Jesus exercised much training with Peter to bring him out of the religious and materialistic concept and into the dominion of God.

You should learn a lesson from Peter's experience. Whatever the Lord says, do it. Whatever the Lord says, take it. Whatever the Lord says, stand on it. You do not need to exercise any reasoning. You do not need to be religious or spiritual. You need to be under God's dominion.

OUR NEED FOR CHRIST AS LIFE

In Genesis 1 we see man with God's image and God's dominion. Then in Genesis 2 there is the tree of life (v. 9). By reading through the Bible, we know that the tree of life is a symbol of Christ. Christ is the tree of life. John 1:4a says, "In Him was life," and 10:10b says, "I have come that they may have life and may have it abundantly." In John 14:6a the Lord said, "I am...the life." Also, in John 15 He said that He is the vine tree. Christ is the tree and the life. Therefore, Christ is the tree of life.

Thus, besides these two words *image* and *dominion,* we have another crucial word—*life.* In order to do anything, we need the proper life. A dog barks because it has the dog life, which is a barking life. A cat is capable in catching mice because of the capacity in the cat life, but we do not have this capacity. Likewise, if we want to express God and exercise God's authority, we need the life to do it. The human life is good neither for expressing God nor for exercising God's authority. But the human life is good for receiving another life that is capable of expressing God and representing God. All the animal lives, such as the dog life, the cat life, or the bird life, are not good for receiving another life. God did not create them in this way. But God did create us in a way that we can receive another life. This life is the eternal life of God Himself, which is Christ.

God created us with a human spirit as the receiving organ to receive God Himself into us as our very life. The human life is not capable of expressing God and not good for exercising God's authority. But the human life is good for one thing, that is, for receiving the life which is capable—the eternal life (1 John 1:2). "He who has the Son has the life; he who does not have the Son of God does not have the life" (5:12). This is the unique life signified by the tree of life.

Christ came and presented Himself to His disciples as life. He told the people that He came that they might have life and might have it abundantly (John 10:10b). In Matthew the message is, "Repent, for the kingdom of the heavens has drawn near" (3:2). But in John the message is, "Unless one is born anew, he cannot see the kingdom of God" (3:3). Matthew and John both deal with the kingdom. Matthew deals with the kingdom as a kind of requirement or demand on us. If we seek to have the kingdom of the heavens, we have to fulfill its requirements. When we read Matthew 5—7, we may want to give up, because what the Lord says here is impossible for us to carry out by our human life. When someone slaps you on your cheek, would you be willing to turn to him your other cheek (5:39)? I am afraid that you would fight back right away. This means that you are not in Matthew but in the law of Moses (v. 38).

After Matthew we must come to the Gospel of John. John also deals with the kingdom, not with its requirements but with the fulfillment of its requirements. The fulfillment of the requirements of the kingdom is Christ as life. You cannot make it, but when Christ comes into you, He will make it. Matthew requires and demands, whereas John affords and supplies. If you have never come to know how much Matthew requires of you for the kingdom, you will never appreciate how much John affords you to meet the requirements of the kingdom. Matthew comes first, and then John follows. Matthew requires so much of us, causing all of us to be disappointed. But in John the Lord comes and says to us, "Don't be disappointed. I am here. I can give you the supply to meet Matthew's demand on you. Whatever Matthew requires of you, I can make it for you."

Do you think that you can express God? Do you think that you can exercise God's authority? You need a higher life, even the highest life. You need Christ. Christ is the life (John 14:6; Col. 3:4), not the teaching. No teaching can make you turn your other cheek to your striker. But there is One who is the life and who is able to do it in you. This One is Christ. "Unless one is born anew, he cannot see the kingdom of God" (John 3:3). Once we have been born anew and have Christ as life, we see the kingdom, the dominion, the authority, of God. Spontaneously, whatever we are, do, and say expresses God.

Therefore, without Christ everything is empty. Without Christ everything is vanity. Man is the meaning of the universe, and Christ is the meaning of human life. Although man is the meaning of the universe, without Christ man has no content or reality. Without Christ man is merely an empty vessel. Man as an empty vessel needs Christ as the content. This is why we have to open up ourselves to Christ and receive Him as our life. Praise the Lord that many of us have done this. But the problem is this—after receiving Christ, we do not live by Christ. We still live by ourselves. Suppose you go to the beach and are rejected and persecuted by someone. If you reason in your mind, you will get into the law of Moses. Instead of reasoning in your mind, you need to say, "O Lord." When you call on the Lord's name, you get into the Gospel of John. The very Christ who is your life will become so vital to you.

Hence, we all have to practice one thing, that is, not to live by ourselves but to always live by Christ. To live by Christ you need to forget about being religious and spiritual. You need to open up yourself all the time and call on His name. Do not keep anything religious or spiritual in your mind. Then you will see that He is the instant, present, up-to-date, moment-by-moment Christ. He is the Christ at this moment.

At the moment when people reject and persecute you, He is the Christ. Do not keep so many doctrines in your mind. Doctrines do not work. Only Christ works. This Christ is the living Christ. He is not the doctrinal Christ or the Christ in teachings, but the Christ who is so present, real, and practical as the life-giving Spirit (1 Cor. 15:45b). Simply call upon Him.

In conclusion, we need to keep in mind that for us to express God and to exercise His authority, we need Christ as life. We also need to realize that Christ today is the life-giving Spirit. He is the living Spirit who is with us all the time. He is present, prevailing, available, and instant. No matter where you are, no matter what situation you are in, whether you are dealing with someone or you are being dealt with by someone, forget about yourself and your reasonings; simply open to Him and call, "O Lord Jesus." Just enjoy Him. He is your life and your content. He is the meaning of your human life.

CHAPTER FIVE

THE CHURCH AS
THE EXPRESSION OF CHRIST

Scripture Reading: Eph. 1:22-23; 5:25-27; 2:15-16, 21-22; 4:11-12; 3:21; 1 Cor. 12:12; Rev. 1:11; Eph. 3:10-11

The first main figure revealed in the Bible is God. Christ is the second main figure. In this chapter we come to the last two main figures in the Bible—the church and the churches.

GOD'S PURPOSE TO HAVE THE CHURCH

According to the divine revelation of the Bible, the church is a matter of God's eternal purpose. God is a God of purpose. He is not a God of nonsense. He is not a meaningless God. Consider yourself. You were made in the image of God, and you are a person with purpose. We are men of purpose because we were made according to God, who is a God of purpose.

God's main purpose is to have the church. God created the heavens, the earth, and billions of other items, and then He created man. God created all things for man, and then God created man for the church. Thus, the church is the center of the universe. In the first chapter I said that man is the center of the universe. That is right. However, man, the corporate man, as the center of the universe is for the church because eventually the church comes into being out of man. Hence, the church is the ultimate center of the universe. This is according to God's eternal purpose which He made in Christ (Eph. 3:10-11). The church is of God's purpose, and God's purpose is for the church.

CHRIST DYING FOR THE CHURCH

In Christianity we all have heard innumerable times that

Christ loved us and died on the cross for us. But most of us have not heard a message telling us that Christ loved the church and died for the church. Ephesians 5:25 says, "Christ also loved the church and gave Himself up for her." Christ loved the church, not just the individuals but a corporate Body, and He gave Himself up for the church. The death of Christ was for the church.

CHRIST'S ATTAINMENTS AND ACCOMPLISHMENTS BEING FOR THE CHURCH

Ephesians 1 says that Christ was raised from the dead and seated in the heavenlies (v. 20). He had all things subjected under His feet and was given to be Head over all things to the church (v. 22). The resurrection of Christ, the ascension of Christ, the enthronement of Christ, and the glorification of Christ are all for the church. All the main items of Christ's attainments and accomplishments—His death, resurrection, ascension, enthronement, and glorification—are for the church.

ALL THE GIFTED PERSONS BEING FOR THE BUILDING UP OF THE CHURCH

We are too self-centered. We are always concerned about our personal salvation. But we have to realize that our personal salvation is for a corporate church. Ephesians 4 says that when Christ ascended to the height, He led a train of vanquished foes and gave gifts to men (v. 8). He made all the vanquished foes the gifts. The apostle Paul was one of these vanquished foes. When he was Saul of Tarsus, he was a real foe to Christ (Acts 8:1, 3). But Christ vanquished him and made this vanquished foe, Saul of Tarsus, the biggest gift. Christ gave this biggest gift, the apostle Paul, to the church for the building up of the Body of Christ. All the gifts, the gifted persons, such as the apostles, prophets, evangelists, and shepherds and teachers, are for the building up of the Body of Christ (Eph. 4:11-12).

GOD PUTTING SATAN TO SHAME THROUGH THE CHURCH

Ephesians 3:10 says, "In order that now to the rulers and

the authorities in the heavenlies the multifarious wisdom of God might be made known through the church." This means that God puts Satan with all his power of darkness to shame through the church. God would say to Satan, "Satan, look at the church. You gave Me a lot of trouble, but out of all the troubles, I have obtained a church. All the troubles you gave Me became a kind of help to Me. So I am wiser than you. Satan, have you seen My wisdom?" Satan caused so many young people to become hippies. But out of the hippies, God has gained a number of saved saints. God is wiser than Satan. It is through the church that the multifarious wisdom of God is made known. Therefore, here we have to be bold enough to say that even Satan is for the church.

Satan always has been and still is trying his best to damage the church. But all the damage caused by Satan is used by God in His wisdom to build up the church. Satan is a tool used by God for the church. If Satan had never come into existence, everything in the universe would be wonderful. There would not be anything evil. Consequently, there would be no tears, no pain, and no suffering. We have to realize that God, in His marvelous wisdom, allowed all the negative things to happen for this one purpose, that is, to produce a wonderful thing—the church. We will need eternity to understand how much good the darkness, suffering, pain, and tears have done for us. Even the dark and negative things are used by God for the church.

THE GLORY OF GOD BEING FOR THE CHURCH

Ephesians 3:21 says, "To Him be the glory in the church." The glory of God is not only in the church but also for the church.

Thus, we see that God's purpose is for the church. Christ's death is for the church. Christ's resurrection, ascension, enthronement, and glorification are for the church. In other words, all the main things accomplished by Christ are for the church. Furthermore, the gifts are for the church. Then Satan, with all the negative things, is for the church. Finally, God's glory is for the church.

THE CHURCH BEING CHRIST

My burden in this chapter is mainly to fellowship with you concerning the church being Christ. First Corinthians 12:12 fully, clearly, and definitely reveals that the church is Christ. This verse says, "Even as the body is one and has many members, yet all the members of the body, being many, are one body, so also is the Christ."

When we say that the church is Christ, this Christ is not an individual Christ but a corporate Christ. This corporate Christ, who is the church, is the expression of the individual Christ. In the four Gospels there is the individual Christ, but in Acts and the Epistles, there is the corporate Christ, the church.

What does it mean to say that the corporate Christ is the church? Let me illustrate. We all are members of the Body of Christ. Suppose we all come together to have a meeting. You come with yourself, another brother comes with himself, and I come with myself. We all come here with ourselves. Thus, we are just a group of "selves" coming together. But if you come with Christ, I come with Christ, and he comes with Christ, we are Christ—not the individual Christ but the corporate Christ. We have people from every tribe, tongue, people, and nation gathered together (Rev. 5:9) as the church. If they live by Christ, then when they come together, they are the church.

We all have to see what the church is. The church is the corporate Body, which is Christ Himself. The church is the totality of all the saints with Christ added together. The church is not a church building. Christ with His church has been confined by the church building for many centuries. But He is being released from the confinement of the church's building.

Furthermore, the church is not an organization of many so-called Christians. The church is Christ Himself. In order to have the church in reality, we need to live by Christ. In chapter 3 we saw that we have to take Christ not only as our life but also as our person. If each one of us takes Christ as his person, not living by himself but by Christ, then each one is Christ. So whenever we come together, we come not with ourselves but with Christ. You come with Christ, and I come with Christ. We all come with Christ. Therefore, the church is Christ.

NO ORDINANCES IN THE CHURCH

I am also burdened to share with you that in the church there are no ordinances. We have seen that we all are Christ, so we all are one Body (Eph. 2:16), which is Christ (1 Cor. 12:12). But look at today's situation in Christianity. We see divisions there, not the one Body. We Christians have been and still are divided. Ephesians 2:15-16 tells us that when Christ in His flesh was dying on the cross, He slew the enmity.

Most of us have heard that on the cross Christ took away our sins, and some of us probably also have heard that on the cross Christ crucified our old man and defeated Satan. But here in Ephesians 2:15-16 we are told that Christ on the cross slew the enmity. The enmity here is caused by the ordinances. Verse 15 speaks of the law of the commandments in ordinances, which create the enmity. Then verse 16 says that Christ has slain the enmity. That means that He has slain all the ordinances.

In Ephesians 2:15 the ordinances are the ways of living and religion. The religious people always have their way of living according to their way of religion. In ancient times the Jews had many ordinances. They had to be circumcised on the eighth day, they had to keep the Sabbath every week, and they had to observe their dietary regulations three times a day. These were the main ordinances of the Jews in ancient times. Due to these ordinances, no Jew would associate with any Gentile. On the other hand, the Gentiles also had their way of living. Therefore, all the different ordinances created enmity between the Jews and the Gentiles.

However, Christ created a Body, a new man, of many different people, not only of the Jews but also of the Gentiles. The new man, the church, the Body of Christ, was created with all kinds of people, who have their particular ways of living. The Americans have their American way, the British have their British way, the Chinese have their Chinese way, and the Japanese have their Japanese way. Even with the Americans, the Yankees have their way, and the Texans have their way. All have different ways of living, different ordinances.

I am afraid that most of you have your own ordinances, ordinances not made by Moses but by yourself. You have your self-made ordinances. Furthermore, there are locally-made ordinances among the local churches, such as a Los Angeles ordinance, a Houston ordinance, a San Francisco ordinance, or a Chicago ordinance. One time in a meeting while some of the attendants were excited, some others walked out. No doubt, they did not agree with what was going on in the meeting. We have to be flexible. If we are not flexible, whatever way we have for our meeting becomes an ordinance. If those dissenting ones who walked out insist on not having a certain way of meeting, that means they have a strong ordinance. If the ones who stayed insist on having their way of meeting, they also become a people with a strong ordinance.

The problem today is that we Christians are always self-centered and self-concerned. We do not see the Body or realize that the Body is all-inclusive. In today's situation everybody has his own choice according to his own taste. A brother may like everything to be nice, quiet, and in a good order in the meeting. He may want all the men to wear ties and all the ladies to be modestly dressed. He wants everyone to come into the meeting one by one and be seated in an orderly way. This is this brother's taste, so he tries to find such a meeting. Thus, that becomes his choice according to his taste. On the other hand, there is another brother who also has his own taste. He likes meetings that are unrestricted and noisy. So he would also travel around to find a meeting where everybody is so free to dress the way he wants and shout and be excited. Eventually, he will find a meeting of his choice according to his taste. This is the situation today.

All these different tastes create trouble, and all the different choices cause divisions. We may like a certain kind of meeting, but we should not make that a choice for ourselves. Brothers and sisters, the church life is not up to our choice.

The church is our destiny. Let us consider two brothers who were born into the same family and have the same family name. The family name is not a matter of choice but a matter of destiny. We all have to see that the church is not a choice but a destiny. If we see this, many problems will be spontaneously solved.

Furthermore, whether or not these two brothers like each other, they are still brothers. The brotherhood is not up to your choice. It is also a matter of destiny. If the first one does not like the second one, he cannot blame the second one but can only go to blame his parents. If you do not like a brother, do not blame him. You have to go to the heavens to blame the Father. That is your destiny. He is a brother to you in your destiny. No matter how you feel, you have to love him. Friendship is a matter of choice, but brotherhood is not. Brotherhood is a matter of destiny.

In the church we have brotherhood, not friendship. Suppose you are a brother in Atlanta. Perhaps one day some of the other brothers in Atlanta would mistreat you. If you decide to give them up, that proves you do not know what the church is. The church is a matter of destiny, and so is the brotherhood. If you see this, you will realize that in the Body of Christ there should not be any ordinances. I may like to be quiet, but being quiet should not be my ordinance. I may like to be noisy, but being noisy should not be my choice. We all have to learn to be general, realizing that the church life is our destiny.

The Lord Jesus has abolished all the ordinances and has slain the enmity. Thus, He can make us all one. Look at the situation when we all gather together. We have many different kinds of people, yet we can all meet together as one. This is the church. There is no such thing as a Puerto Rican church, a Mexican church, a Japanese church, a Chinese church, a Texan church, a Californian church, or an Anglican church. There is simply the one church, which is the unique Body of Christ. The Lord is going to recover this. Without this being recovered, it will be difficult for Him to come back. We all have to see that the church is Christ, and this corporate Christ includes all kinds of real Christians.

Do not put demands on others. As long as someone is a dear brother in the Lord, that is good enough. No matter what he does in the meeting, you have to love him because he is a brother in Christ. Remember that you do not have a choice. If you have seen the church, you will lose all the choices. Do not think that I am an easygoing person. But by His mercy and by His grace, I can say that I am happy with all of the brothers. As long as one is a brother, we all have to be happy with him. Are you ready to give up all your choices? Maybe some of you are always nice and quiet. But the Lord will bring a lot of people who are noisy and who like to jump and shout, "O Lord! Amen! Hallelujah!" If you decide to drop the church because you dislike the noisy ones, this means that you are keeping your choice and giving up your destiny.

What I am fellowshipping with you is not a small matter. By His mercy and grace, we have to be happy with all genuine Christians. As long as they are brothers and sisters in the Lord, we have to say, "Hallelujah!" If some like to shout, we should shout with them. But if we like to be quiet, the ones who like to shout should also be willing to be quiet with us. You should not demand that I shout with you yet refuse to be quiet with me. Neither should I demand that you be quiet with me yet refuse to shout with you. It must be fair. Eventually, we will all say, "We do not care for shouting or for being quiet; we care only for Christ."

This is the way to have the church life. No one insists on anything. All the leading ones and all the leaders of the different groups here in Los Angeles can testify that throughout the years none among us has ever insisted on anything. We have always been open to one another unto the Lord. We have no regulations. This is why we are changing over the years. Someone said, "Oh, the church in Los Angeles is changing so fast. If you go away for two months and come back, it will be absolutely different." They are right. Because we do not have regulations, we keep changing, or it is better to say that we are always improving.

We have no regulations, no rituals, no forms, and therefore no ordinances. Sometimes I heard some brothers say, "I think the Chinese people won't like this." Immediately, I advised them not to say that. If you say that, it means you are keeping a kind of Chinese ordinance. In the church we have no ordinance. We have only Christ. Since this is the case, we can easily have the oneness. This is why many visitors in the past years were deeply impressed with the oneness of the church in Los Angeles. By His mercy, there are no ordinances in the church here. This is the main point in the Lord's recovery. The Lord is going to recover the proper church life, not only in Los Angeles but also throughout the world. But this needs all of us to have a strong realization that there should not be any kind of ordinance.

THE LOCAL CHURCHES

We have seen that the church is the Body of Christ and the expression of Christ. Now we need to realize that this church as the Body of Christ needs the local churches. The church is the expression of Christ, and the local churches are the expression of the church. Without the local churches you cannot contact the church. The church is embodied in the local churches. The church is also realized and experienced in the local churches. So for the practical church life, we all need the local churches. In the Lord's recovery the local churches are also a main point.

No doubt, in the New Testament the church as the Body of Christ has been fully revealed. Yet if you read through Acts and the Epistles to the last book of the New Testament, Revelation, you will see that the church is fully expressed in the local churches. In the last book of the Bible, what you see is not the church but the local churches. In Revelation 1:11 the apostle John heard a voice saying to him, "What you see write in a scroll and send it to the seven churches: to Ephesus and to Smyrna and to Pergamos and to Thyatira and to Sardis and to Philadelphia and to Laodicea." Here are seven churches in seven cities—one church for one city and one city with only one church. These are the local churches. Today the Lord is recovering the local churches. Wherever we go, we are the one local church there. If we go to Houston, we are the one local church in Houston. If we go to Anaheim, we are the one local church in Anaheim. The same is true if we go to San Francisco, Seattle, or anywhere else.

BEING BUILT UP IN THE LOCAL CHURCHES

By being kept, preserved, in the local churches, we are being built up. In the local churches we can be built up. If you have your own choice, you do not keep your destiny. When you like this group of Christians, you stay with them. When you feel unhappy with them, you say goodbye to them and go somewhere else. If that is the case, how can you be built up? We all know what it is to be built up. Look at any building. Many pieces of material are all fitly framed together. That is a building. Ephesians 2:21-22 says, "In whom [Christ Jesus] all the building, being fitted together, is growing into a holy temple in the Lord; in whom you also are being built together into a dwelling place of God in spirit." *In whom you also* means that we local saints are also being built together. Wherever we go, wherever we are, we have to be the one local church in that locality. Then by being so preserved, we surely will learn the lesson and will spontaneously be built up together.

Since I am now living in Los Angeles, I have to be a brother in the church in Los Angeles. Whether I like you or not, I cannot escape. I have to stay with you. This is my destiny. Therefore, I have to learn the lesson. I have to be dealt with. Even I have to be broken. I have to be transformed so that I may be built up with you. If we all are like this, we all will be built up in the local churches.

Forget about being religious or being "spiritual." Just take care of one thing—be in a local church and be built up with others. Whether you are religious or not, whether you are spiritual or not, does not mean much to the Lord. What matters to Him is whether or not you are in a local church being built up with others. This is the unique thing that the Lord is after today.

In summary, what are the four points that we want to stress in this chapter? First, the church is Christ. Second, there are no ordinances in the church. Third, the local churches are the expression of the church—one church, one city. This is the only way and the only ground for us to keep the oneness and have the proper church life. Fourth, we need to be built up in the local church. As long as we are built up in the local church, we are in the Lord's will, we are in the Lord's recovery, and we are under the preparation for His coming back.

CHAPTER SIX

THE CHURCH LIFE AS
THE REAL COMMUNAL LIFE

Scripture Reading: Rom. 12:10; John 13:34-35; 15:16-17

In the previous chapters we saw three things: first, man is the center of the universe; second, Christ is the meaning of human life; and third, the church is the expression of Christ. Now in this chapter our burden is to see the real communal life.

THE GOD-CREATED DESIRE
TO HAVE A COMMUNAL LIFE

Today not only in the United States but also in many countries on this earth, the young people are desiring to have some kind of communal life. This desire comes out of our natural makeup. In our natural makeup, in our natural life, there is a kind of desire to have a community where we may live together with others.

Suppose you have everything. You have education, money, the best house, and the best car. You have obtained the best of everything. Yet if you were told to go up to the top of a high mountain and live there by yourself, would you do it? None of us would do it because, even though we may have the best things, we would be too lonely by ourselves. We human beings need to be in a community. Hence, this desire to have a communal life is something in our makeup. God created man in this way.

In Genesis 1:26 God first said, "Let Us make man," and then He said, "Let them have dominion." *Man* is singular, but *them,* the pronoun for *man,* is plural. Did God make one man or many men? People think it is easy to understand the Bible.

Yes, on the one hand, the Bible is simple. But on the other hand, it is really hard for people to understand. Why did God use the singular noun *man* and then the plural pronoun *them*? Did He make one man or many men? The answer is: God made many men in one man. Or you can say that God made one man with many men. This simply means that in God's intention, man is corporate. God did not create an Adam, then an Abraham, then a David, etc. God created a corporate man—one man with all men. In God's intention, what He did was a corporate thing. So we all have to realize that the desire to have a communal life was something created in the human nature by God.

Every human being in his human nature has a desire to live with others. Consider the children in your neighborhood. If you try to confine each one of them in their houses, you will bring a great suffering to them. They like to go out to make friends. They like to be in a community. God created man with a nature and a desire to have a communal life as a preparation for the church life. The church life is a communal life, a corporate life. The church life is a life of a proper community.

Let me use a little illustration. Many times you feel thirsty. What is thirst? Thirst is a feeling caused by a desire for a drink. Suppose you do not have a desire for any drink, yet I ask you to drink; that would be a punishment to you. You would suffer a lot. But since God created in you a desire to drink so that you have such a thirst, you will be happy to drink without anyone forcing you.

Likewise, in God's creation God created us with a desire for a communal life. Due to the fall, however, this communal life was spoiled and damaged when the human race came to the time of Babel (Gen. 11:1-9). *Babel* means "confusion." At Babel many different languages came in and caused the human race to be divided. Consequently, there came in the hatred, the enmity, between different peoples with different languages.

In the New Testament the Lord Jesus accomplished redemption to bring people back to God's original purpose. Acts 2 tells us that on the day of Pentecost all the different people of different languages became one (vv. 5-11). They were brought back to the original state of oneness. This was not just a recovery but a re-creation. Ephesians 2:15-16 tells us that Christ on the cross abolished all the ordinances and slew the enmity among people for the purpose of creating a new man.

The Bible tells us that first God created one man, and then Christ created a new man. In the Bible there are two creations: the old creation of God and the new creation of Christ. In His old creation God created a man; in His new creation Christ created a new man.

Brothers and sisters, we have to realize that in the new man created by Christ, we have something in common. First, in the new man we have a common life. In Christ we all have the same life, and with this common life we have a common nature and a common desire. After we are saved, immediately within us there is a desire to contact some genuine Christians for fellowship. This is the desire for a community, a communal life. The church life is the real communal life.

CHRIST AS OUR COMMON ELEMENT, LIFE, AND PERSON FOR US TO LOVE ONE ANOTHER

We have to know that if we want to have a certain living, we need a certain life. God created man with a life that desires to be in a community, but that life was damaged and poisoned. Look at the situation of human society today. On the one hand, people like to live together. But on the other hand, people have become very selfish. You want to live in a community, yet you always have problems with those in your neighborhood. You want to have schoolmates, classmates, roommates, and office mates, but eventually you fight with them. You even fight with your own brothers and sisters. Thus, on the one hand, because we have the God-created nature, we have the desire to live with others; on the other hand, because our human life was damaged and spoiled by Satan, in our fallen nature we do not have the proper life for communal living.

But now we have Christ. Christ is wonderful. He is the common factor, the common element, for us to be one in the communal life with love for one another (Rom. 12:10). I do not know the names of all the brothers, but I still love them very much simply because they are brothers in the Lord. There is a common element among all the brothers, and that element is Christ. Christ is the element that causes us to love one another. Also, Christ within us is the life with the ability for us to love one another.

Do you believe that human beings today can really love one another? It is impossible. If you put a large number of people together for even a short period of time, there will be arguing and fighting. But when we Christians come together and realize that we have Christ within us, immediately we have a wonderful love for one another. For Christians to love is easy, but for Christians to hate is rather hard. Generally speaking, young people are always disgusted with old people. But it is hard for a young man as a Christian to hate an older brother in Christ. As an older brother, I love the young brothers and sisters so much. This is because we all have Christ. There is something common within us. Whenever I meet someone and find out that he is a brother, something within me leaps because we have a common element, a common factor. We are able, capable, and qualified to have the communal life.

However, Satan not only damaged the old man in God's old creation; he also tried and is still trying to damage the new man in Christ. Even to some extent, he has been successful in this matter. Many Christians have been damaged and divided by ordinances. This is why the Lord has brought us into His recovery where we are open to Him and to one another. I am convinced that the Lord is going to recover the proper church life to meet the need of many people. We need to tell the unbelievers that the way to have the proper communal life is to receive Christ and get into the church.

We brothers and sisters here in Los Angeles, in a sense, are communal. But in another sense, we are still short of the communal life. Hence, the Lord has to work deeper in us so that we may have more love for one another. In John 13:34-35 the Lord told the disciples, "A new commandment I give to you, that you love one another, even as I have loved you, that you also love one another. By this shall all men know that you are My disciples, if you have love for one another." What is the sign of our being Christians, of our being disciples of Christ? The sign is the brotherly love, the love among the brothers for one another. We have to love one another.

Furthermore, in John 15:16-17 the Lord Jesus said, "You did not choose Me, but I chose you, and I set you that you should go forth and bear fruit...These things I command you that you may love one another." The Lord has chosen us and charged us to bear fruit by our loving one another. If we love one another, many people will be brought in. If the young people among us love one another in Christ and with Christ, many young people will be brought in. The best way to have the gospel outreach is to love one another. The best way to bear fruit is to love one another. The best way to bring people in is to love one another.

But how can we love one another? We can love one another only by taking Christ as our person and our life. To say this is simple, but to put this into practice is not so simple. If four brothers come together to live in the same house as roommates, they all need to take Christ as their person. If any of them fails to take Christ as his person, he will become the biggest problem to the other brothers. As long as you take Christ as your person, you will be so lovable. Then there will be no problem. Do not put a demand on others. You have to put the demand on yourself and take Christ as your person and your life.

Brothers and sisters, from now on, the Lord is going to do a new thing to release Himself from the confinement of fallen Christianity and to release His church from all kinds of ordinances. Furthermore, He will do a new thing in causing us to love one another even to the extent that we will be one in our living. Then people will say, "These are the disciples of Christ. This is what I have been looking for." This is what God is after, and this is also what human beings are after. This is the church life as the real communal life.

CHAPTER SEVEN

"GO THEREFORE AND DISCIPLE
ALL THE NATIONS"

Scripture Reading: Matt. 28:16-20; Acts 1:8; 13:1-3; 14:23, 26-27

In this chapter we come to the last point of the burden for this book. This point is, "Go therefore and disciple all the nations" (Matt. 28:19a). The Greek word for *nations* may also be rendered as "Gentiles." As we are getting ourselves prepared to go and disciple the nations, we need certain qualifications. We need to be qualified in certain aspects.

GOING TO THE LAND OF THE GENTILES

The Lord did not charge His disciples to go and disciple the nations in the temple. He appointed them to go to Galilee. In Matthew 4 we are told that Galilee was the land of the Gentiles; it was called "Galilee of the Gentiles" (v. 15). The Lord told the disciples to get out of the so-called Holy Land and go to the land of the Gentiles.

THE NEED TO BE TRANSCENDENT

Moreover, the Lord's charge to His disciples took place on a mountain (28:16). This is quite meaningful. To be outside of the temple, outside of the synagogues, outside of the religious centers, and to be on the mountaintop simply means that you have to be on high ground. You have to be transcendent. You have to be on the top of the high mountain to see the nations.

Young brothers and sisters, if you have the intention to go and disciple the unbelievers, you have to be on high. You have to be on the top of the high mountain to look down at the pitiful, miserable situation. When the Lord Jesus was on this earth, no doubt, many times He was on the seashore, on the beach. But when He gave the commandment to the disciples to go and disciple others, He did not do it on the beach. He did it on the top of a high mountain. If we are going to disciple others, first, we have to be on high. If we are on the same level as the Americans, we are finished. We have to be on high to disciple others.

THE LORD HAVING ALL AUTHORITY
IN HEAVEN AND ON EARTH

Next, in Matthew 28:18 the Lord Jesus said, "All authority has been given to Me in heaven and on earth." Some versions use the word *power* instead of *authority,* but the Greek word here means "authority." Authority is higher than power. Let me illustrate in this way. On the street, there are policemen and there are cars. A big car driving on the road has the power, whereas a little policeman has the authority. No matter how powerful your car is, you have to come under the authority of the policeman. Thus, authority is above power. Jesus has not only power but also authority. Both in heaven and on earth the authority belongs to Jesus.

Jesus has the authority over the United States, over the Middle East, and over the whole earth. Jesus has the authority, not the government of the United States, nor the government of Russia, nor the government of China. Jesus is above every nation (Rev. 1:5). We have to see that Jesus has been given all authority in heaven and on earth. Then when we go, we go with the authority of the ascended, enthroned, and glorified Jesus.

BEING IN THE TRIUNE GOD
TO PUT OTHERS INTO THE TRIUNE GOD

Matthew 28:19 also shows us that when we go to disciple others, we need to have the realization that we are in the Triune God. We not only have the authority of Jesus but also are one with Jesus. We are in the Triune God. We are not going to teach others some religion. We are going to baptize them into the Triune God.

According to the grammatical construction of Matthew 28:19, to disciple the nations is by baptizing them. You have to baptize them into something. To baptize is to dip. If I baptize my eyeglasses, this means that I dip them into something else. Likewise, if I am going to baptize someone, this means that I am going to put him into something else. When we baptize others, we put them into the Triune God. To disciple the nations is to baptize them into God, to put them into God.

If you are going to put others into God, you surely need to be in God first. Then you can tell others that you are in the Triune God and that you want to put them into the Triune God. You could say, "I have no intention to put you into Christianity. I have no intention to put you into any denomination, any sect, or any group. My intention is to put you into the Triune God, in whom I am. I am in the Triune God, and I am going to put you into the Triune God, in whom I am." This is different from the preaching of the gospel in a low way. You need to have the realization and the assurance that you are putting people into God, because you are in God.

HAVING POWER TO PREACH THE HIGH GOSPEL

We need power to preach the high gospel. In Luke 24:49 the Lord told the disciples to "stay in the city until you put on power from on high." And in Acts 1:8 He said, "You shall receive power when the Holy Spirit comes upon you." When the power from on high comes upon us, we will be qualified and equipped for witnessing unto the uttermost part of the earth. If you mean business with the Lord, and if today you are high on the top of a mountain, realizing that all authority is His and that you are really in the Triune God, then you already have the power. You just need to claim it. When you go to the young people, you have to tell the universe, "I have the power!" You should have this kind of faith. Do not care for your feeling or for your experiences. You have to care for the Word of God. When you go to disciple the unbelievers, you need to have the faith that you are in the power.

THE NEED TO BE BUILT WITH OTHERS

Another thing that I want to fellowship with you is that

you need to be built with others. The Lord Jesus did not tell us as individuals to go to the nations. His charge was a corporate charge. The ones who go are the church in a corporate sense. This means that we need to be fully built together with others in a practical church. If you young brothers are not built together, that means you are fully defeated. If you are not built together, you are not on high, not on the top of a mountain. Rather, you are in the lowest place, in the valley of Jericho. As long as you are not built together with others, you are low, you are through with the authority of Christ, you are outside of the Triune God, and you do not have the faith to claim the power. Many Christians try their best to preach the gospel, yet their preaching is powerless because they are not built together with others.

Before the day of Pentecost, there were about a hundred and twenty gathered together (Acts 1:15). They were built together as one man. Then on the day of Pentecost, when Peter stood up, another eleven stood with him (2:14). They all stood together. Peter was only the mouthpiece of the Body. Suppose five of you young brothers would go to the beach to disciple the unbelievers. You have to realize that it is not only five of you going but also the whole church going with you. You should have the assurance that you are members of the moving Body, the "going" church. When you go, the whole church goes with you. This is why you need to be built together.

When the Lord Jesus was on this earth, before He went to be crucified, a contention arose among the disciples as to which of them seemed to be greatest (Luke 22:24). I am afraid that some of you have the thought that you want to be a leader, to be the greatest. If we have this thought, we cannot be built up with others. Have you really been built up together as one? Others may not know where you are, but all the demons know where you are. The devil knows, and he would tell you, "Don't cheat me, I know where you are. You are not one. You have never been built up together. You can cheat others, but you can't cheat me."

You all have to realize that man is the center of the universe, and Christ is the meaning of your human life. Moreover, the church is the real expression of Christ, and this church life is the real communal life. This communal life is a life with a group of believers built together as one in Christ and with Christ. Can you tell the enemy from your pure conscience that you are really built up together as one in Christ and with Christ? If you lose this, you lose everything. When we are built up as one, we have the power and the authority.

Acts 13 says that in the church in Antioch there were prophets and teachers (v. 1). At that time there was a real building up in the church in Antioch. It was not that Paul and Barnabas were praying in their home, and in their morning watch they received guidance and inspiration from the Lord. Acts 13 tells us, first of all, that Paul and Barnabas were in the church. People may talk about the church, but their talk is something in the air. Paul and Barnabas were in a church in a definite locality, in Antioch. If you are going to do a prevailing work for the preaching of the gospel, you have to be built up in a local church, in a church which is practical and definite.

In the church which was in Antioch, there were five prophets and teachers who were built into the church. The guidance from the Holy Spirit came to them as representatives of the church (v. 2). Verse 3 says that three of them sent out Barnabas and Saul, but verse 4 says that Barnabas and Saul were sent out by the Holy Spirit. This proves that the three were one with the Spirit in the Lord's move, and the Spirit honored their sending as His. They were one with the Spirit and had the Spirit's leading because they were built into the church.

You all need to be built together in the church. Then in the church you will get the guidance, and from the church you will go out, not to do some mere preaching work but to produce and establish the local churches. The two sent ones, Paul and Barnabas, went out to preach the gospel, but their preaching was for the producing and establishing of the local churches. Wherever they went, they preached. Wherever they preached, a local church was established in that locality. So the Bible tells us that Paul and Barnabas, on their return journey, appointed elders in every church (14:23). They went out from the church, the work they did was for the church, and eventually they came back to the church in Antioch (v. 26). Remember that their work was "from the church, for the church, and back to the church." With them everything was for the church. Their work was not separate, independent, or isolated from the church. In Acts 13 and 14 *church* always means the local church. Acts 13:1 says that the prophets and teachers were "in Antioch, in the local church," and 14:23 speaks of "every church," that is, every local church.

Today's Christian preachers may talk a lot about the church, yet they do not have a local church. Do not just talk about the church in theory. You need to be in a practical, definite church. There may be much discussion about the church, the Body life, the Body ministry, and the New Testament church, but where is it? We need to pray, "O Lord, help us to have the proper church life and to be so definite and practical in the church life."

Without the church life we are finished. As long as the members of our physical body remain in our body, they are beautiful and useful. But when they are isolated, they become terrifying and useless. My two eyes are beautiful as long as they remain in my body. But if they were isolated from my body, they would become ugly and terrifying. When you shake hands with me, you feel so good about my hand. But suppose my hand is isolated from my body and is presented to you. Regardless of how bold you are, you would be terrified. Even a little nose which is useful for breathing becomes useless and frightening if it is separated from the body. Many dear Christians today could be really useful members, but they have become "terrifying" because they are isolated from the Body. Many dear Christians consider themselves so wonderful and marvelous, yet they do not realize that they are terrifying due to their isolation.

Throughout the past years I heard numerous testimonies from different people saying that the most inspiring thing they saw and the deepest impression they received of the church in Los Angeles was the oneness. Only the oneness can convince people that the church is real. How we thank the Lord for so many young people who have been caught by the

Lord in this evil age. You have a heart toward the Lord and have the intention to be used by the Lord. This is really good. But before you go and disciple others, you need to be built up together.

Forget about trying to be a leader. Paul said that he was "less than the least of all saints" (Eph. 3:8). He considered himself smaller than the smallest. We need to be like him. Some Christians are struggling for power, for leadership, in the church. This is shameful. To want to be a leader is not a glory or a boast; it is a shame. In the Gentile world, to be in power is a remarkable thing. But in the church to struggle to be in power is shameful.

I know the story. I am as human as you are. Furthermore, I have passed through your age. Today young people like to have the leadership. You should not have this attitude: "If I am a leader in this, I am for it. If not, I am not for it." If any one of you is like this, you are through. Do not try to be a leader. Instead, by His mercy and grace, just be a member built with others in the church. You all need to be built up together.

Today the worldly people say that union is power. But we say that the building up is power. If you are built up with others, whatever you do will be for the producing of the church life. If not, whatever you do will be for the separating, the dividing, of the Body. What the Lord needs today is a built-up church. He needs a group of members who are built up together so that they can go not only to preach the gospel but also to produce the built-up church life.

The real communal life is a built-up life, a life in which you are built up as one. This is where we have the power. This power is not just to convince others or just to bring others to Christ, but to produce the local churches. In our work there should be nothing personal or individualistic. All the time our work is from the church, for the church, and back to the church.

Do not try to do a quick work. The more you try to be quick, the more you will be slowed down. By His grace and mercy, just be built up together with others. We need to pray, "O Lord, I do not need anything but the building. Grant me to be built up with others, Lord. O Lord, I need the building. I need the oneness." We need to have the realization that we are one and take action to go and disciple the nations.

We have seen that man is the center of the universe, that Christ is the meaning of the human life, that the church is the expression of Christ, and that the real communal life is the church life. When we have the communal life in reality, the building up of the church, we are qualified to go. You need to be built up and then you can go. Wherever you go, there will be a church produced and established. Go from the church, and come back to the church. Throughout all the places where you travel, churches will be established. This is the Lord's purpose.

The following hymn (*Hymns*, #1293) embodies the burden of this book:

1   O I'm a man—
       I'm the meaning of the universe;
    Yes, I'm a man—
       I'm the meaning of the universe.
         God made me such,
         I am so much;
    I'm the center and the meaning of the universe.

2   Christ lives in me—
       He's the meaning of my human life;
    Christ lives in me—
       He's the meaning of my human life.
         Yes, He's in me
         My all to be;
    He's the meaning and reality of my human life.

3   The church is Christ—
       His expression on the earth today;
    The church is Christ—
       His expression on the earth today.
         This corporate man
         Fulfills God's plan,
    That this man may have dominion over all the
         earth.

4 The local church—
    It's the new and real family life;
The local church—
    It's the new and real family life.
      We have the way
      To live today—
Eating, drinking Christ we're built up as the
    local church.

5 What shall we do?
    We should go and tell the world of this.
What shall we do?
    We should go and tell the world of this.
      Disciple all—
      This is our call.
Let us go and spread the news abroad to every
    land.

ABOUT THE AUTHOR

Witness Lee was born in 1905 in northern China and raised in a Christian family. At age 19 he was fully captured for Christ and immediately consecrated himself to preach the gospel for the rest of his life. Early in his service, he met Watchman Nee, a renowned preacher, teacher, and writer. Witness Lee labored together with Watchman Nee under his direction. In 1934 Watchman Nee entrusted Witness Lee with the responsibility for his publication operation, called the Shanghai Gospel Bookroom.

Prior to the Communist takeover in 1949, Witness Lee was sent by Watchman Nee and his other co-workers to Taiwan to ensure that the things delivered to them by the Lord would not be lost. Watchman Nee instructed Witness Lee to continue the former's publishing operation abroad as the Taiwan Gospel Bookroom, which has been publicly recognized as the publisher of Watchman Nee's works outside China. Witness Lee's work in Taiwan manifested the Lord's abundant blessing. From a mere 350 believers, newly fled from the mainland, the churches in Taiwan grew to 20,000 in five years.

In 1962 Witness Lee felt led of the Lord to come to the United States, and he began to minister in Los Angeles. During his 35 years of service in the U.S., he ministered in weekly meetings and weekend conferences, delivering several thousand spoken messages. Much of his speaking has since been published as over 400 titles. Many of these have been translated into over fourteen languages. He gave his last public conference in February 1997 at the age of 91.

He leaves behind a prolific presentation of the truth in the Bible. His major work, *Life-study of the Bible,* comprises over 25,000 pages of commentary on every book of the Bible from the perspective of the believers' enjoyment and experience of God's divine life in Christ through the Holy Spirit. Witness Lee was the chief editor of a new translation of the New Testament into Chinese called the Recovery Version and directed the translation of the same into English. The Recovery Version also appears in a number of other languages. He provided an extensive body of footnotes, outlines, and spiritual cross references. A radio broadcast of his messages can be heard on Christian radio stations in the United States. In 1965 Witness Lee founded Living Stream Ministry, a non-profit corporation, located in Anaheim, California, which officially presents his and Watchman Nee's ministry.

Witness Lee's ministry emphasizes the experience of Christ as life and the practical oneness of the believers as the Body of Christ. Stressing the importance of attending to both these matters, he led the churches under his care to grow in Christian life and function. He was unbending in his conviction that God's goal is not narrow sectarianism but the Body of Christ. In time, believers began to meet simply as the church in their localities in response to this conviction. In recent years a number of new churches have been raised up in Russia and in many European countries.

OTHER BOOKS PUBLISHED BY
Living Stream Ministry

Available at
Christian bookstores, or contact Living Stream Ministry
2431 W. La Palma Ave. • Anaheim, CA 92801
1-800-549-5164 • www.livingstream.com